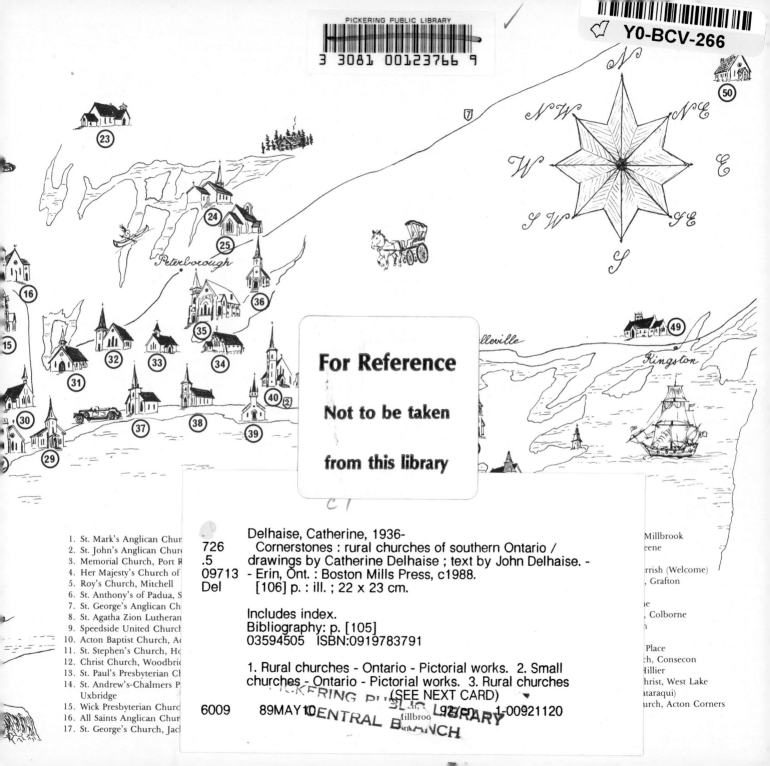

1. St. Mark's Anglican Chur
2. St. John's Anglican Churc
3. Memorial Church, Port R
4. Her Majesty's Church of
5. Roy's Church, Mitchell
6. St. Anthony's of Padua, S
7. St. George's Anglican Ch
8. St. Agatha Zion Lutheran
9. Speedside United Church
10. Acton Baptist Church, Ac
11. St. Stephen's Church, Ho
12. Christ Church, Woodbri
13. St. Paul's Presbyterian Cl
14. St. Andrew's-Chalmers P
   Uxbridge
15. Wick Presbyterian Churc
16. All Saints Anglican Chur
17. St. George's Church, Jac

... Millbrook
... eene

... rrish (Welcome)
..., Grafton

... e
..., Colborne
... h

... Place
... ch, Consecon
... Hillier
... hrist, West Lake
... ataraqui)
... urch, Acton Corners

Delhaise, Catherine, 1936-
    Cornerstones : rural churches of southern Ontario /
drawings by Catherine Delhaise ; text by John Delhaise. -
- Erin, Ont. : Boston Mills Press, c1988.
    [106] p. : ill. ; 22 x 23 cm.

726
.5
09713
Del

Includes index.
Bibliography: p. [105]
03594505   ISBN:0919783791

1. Rural churches - Ontario - Pictorial works. 2. Small
churches - Ontario - Pictorial works. 3. Rural churches
(SEE NEXT CARD)

6009   89MAY10   92/60   1-00921120

CORNERSTONES
RURAL CHURCHES OF SOUTHERN ONTARIO

CORNERSTONES

RURAL CHURCHES OF SOUTHERN ONTARIO

Drawings by Catherine Delhaise
Text by John Delhaise

THE BOSTON MILLS PRESS

To all the rural communities,
may their churches go on being
the cornerstones of their life.

ACKNOWLEDGEMENTS

There is no way we can separately thank all our friends who, for many years, were on the "look out" for little country churches to refer to us. They contributed to making this book more complete and their encouragement was indeed needed during this six-year venture. A special thanks to all the ministers, priests and local people who so willingly compiled the histories of their churches.

ISBN 0-919783-79-1

© Catherine Delhaise, 1988
© John Delhaise, 1988

Published by:
THE BOSTON MILLS PRESS
132 Main Street
Erin, Ontario N0B 1T0
(519) 833-2407

Cover Watercolour:
    St. Anthony's of Padua, Shakespeare, Ontario

Book Design by Gill Stead
Typeset by Speed River Graphics
Printed by Ampersand, Guelph

American Association
for State and Local History
Award of Merit

Winners of the
Heritage Canada
Communications Award

We wish to acknowledge the financial assistance and encouragement of The Canada Council, the Ontario Arts Council and the Office of the Secretary of State.

INTRODUCTION

Cornerstones is a husband-and-wife team venture. Travelling Ontario's rural roads together, Catherine sketched her favourite churches while I gathered historical information from Clergy and local residents. *Cornerstones* is not a book about church history or architecture, not even an exhaustive treatment of its subject, but a book of churches which appeal to Catherine's aesthetic sense. Since she did not want to repeat architectural styles, Catherine had difficulty in selecting which churches to include. Thus, reluctantly, she had to exclude some fine buildings. Some of these churches figured prominently in the nation's history, others, perhaps because of their size or location, less so. My aim was to make an interesting and exciting book which would appeal to a wide readership. The purpose of *Cornerstones* is to document those country churches which were the cornerstones of small communities. Rather than just give a standard history, I preferred to use oral information which, though risking error, had local flavour.

Cornerstones is a result of six years of hard but pleasant work. How did it begin? The stylistic variety exhibited in country churches impressed Catherine, giving rise to the idea for this book.

Most of the churches represented in *Cornerstones* were built in the second half of the nineteenth century. During this period, the church was an integral part of the rural community. It not only supplied the spiritual needs of its members, but also provided a welcome gathering place.

Though Catherine and I sought, in the spirit of ecumenism, to include churches of all denominations, Anglican churches preponderate in *Cornerstones*. Many early Anglican settlers were wealthy and cultivated enough to hire distinguished architects, who designed durable stone churches in one or another of the traditional European styles. Although their congregations dwindled despite the growth in population, the old edifices remained to commemorate the early days of Anglicanism in Canada. By contrast, the first Roman Catholic settlers were neither affluent nor educated, but humble craftsmen and farmers who could ill afford opulent churches. They quickly outgrew their original buildings, replacing them with larger, more modern and often stylish ones. However, these later churches lack antique interest. Since Jewish and other religious communities established themselves in cities, they fall, regrettably, outside the scope of this book.

It is our hope that *Cornerstones* will incite the reader to discover and enjoy more of our Canadian heritage.

John Delhaise

St. Mark's Anglican Church, 1804
NIAGARA-ON-THE-LAKE

ANGLICAN

In 1792 the Rev. Robert Addison arrived from Cambridge as a "missionary to Niagara" and, 12 years later, St. Mark's was built. The British used the church as a hospital during the War of 1812. Rev. Addison conducted the funeral service for General Brock, who died at the Battle of Queenston Heights and who was interred at Fort George. The Americans commandeered the church in 1813 for a hospital and storehouse, only to burn it with the rest of the town. The exterior stone walls alone remained, and after the war the reconstruction slowly began. The church assumed its present shape after 1843.

Before meeting with his provincial cabinet to commemorate the centennial of Canada in 1967, the Honourable John Robarts read the lessons during morning prayer at St. Mark's in this town where the first legislature of Upper Canada convened in 1792. The Queen Mother attended service in the church on the occasion of the Niagara-on-the-Lake bicentennial in October 1981.

The church still has the oldest privately owned library, containing about 1,500 eighteenth-century volumes that Addison brought to Niagara.

Delhaise 83

St. John's Church, 1913
SIMCOE

ANGLICAN

After the American Declaration of Independence in 1776, the United Empire Loyalists moved to Canada in order to stay under British rule. In the late eighteenth century the Rev. R. Addison tended the Loyalists in Simcoe from his headquarters in Newark (now Niagara-on-the-Lake). The parish was so large that it was impossible to minister regularly to the congregation, so services were few. To compensate, the Canon Ussher, in charge of the Chapel of the Mohawks in Brantford, also met here for worship.

A log church was built in 1821, but it burned within a year or two. A new church was built in 1824, but it suffered the same fate. In 1826 the Rev. F. Evans became the first resident clergyman. The present church opened on December 14, 1913.

It is remarkable that so many members of the congregation presented the church with such an abundance of gifts, thus making its interior as attractive as its outside. The frieze-decorated tower and battlements contrast with the picturesque Regency Gothic windows and buttresses.

Delhaise 84

Memorial Church, Est. 1870
PORT RYERSE

ANGLICAN

After the War of Independence many people wanted things to remain British, so they left the United States for Canada. A large number of these immigrants, known as United Empire Loyalists, settled in Ontario. A staunch member of this community, Lt.-Col. Samuel Ryerse, erected a grist mill in 1795, and around this enterprise grew Port Ryerse.

Ryerse Memorial Church was built in memory of Colonel Ryerse. Near the north shore of Lake Erie, this little Loyalist pioneer wooden church, its straight tower decorated with pinnacles, still welcomes many Sunday worshippers, who can be very proud of their beautiful Regency-type altar table.

Her Majesty's Church of the Mohawks, 1785
BRANTFORD

ANGLICAN

The British government gave the Indians the territory "six miles on either side of the Grand River" from its source to its mouth, on which land was later built the first Protestant church in what is now Ontario.

In 1785 Captain Joseph Brant ordered the church's construction, and today it remains on the site of the modern Six Nations Reserve at Brantford. The timbers, cut by hand in Paris, Ontario, were floated down the Grand River, the nails were hand drawn, and the bell, cast in England in 1786, was the first in Upper Canada.

The gold carpet in the sanctuary came from Westminster Abbey, where it lay during the crowning of Queen Elizabeth II.

The Apostle's Creed, the Ten Commandments, and the Lord's Prayer are written in the Mohawk language over the altar. We especially enjoyed the stained glass windows representing Indian scenes. The official designation of Royal Chapel was given in 1904, the only such title in the world belonging to a native people's organization.

Delhaise 84

Roy's Church, 1911
MITCHELL

UNITED

In 1851 farmers built a log church on a piece of land donated by pioneer William Roy.

The log church was replaced by a brick structure in 1872, but the beautiful, patterned red-and-white brick church in existence today was started in 1911.

In the early years people from miles around worshipped there, and it has been said that, in the dusty season, in order to arrive well groomed at church, the young ladies removed their shiny shoes and walked barefoot. Today, in our automobile age, even country people prefer to drive to the city to worship. Roy's congregation had to close its doors.

The church was to be destroyed in 1968, but a family bought and preserved it as a gift shop and tea room called the Country Spire.

Delhaise 83

St. Anthony of Padua, 1863
SHAKESPEARE

ROMAN CATHOLIC

Built with variegated field stones in 1863, St. Athony of Padua replaces a log church and school where, rumour says, the poorly paid teacher kept chickens to supplement his income.

St. Anthony of Padua is a little gem of late-Georgian style. There are so many similarities between this church and St. Agatha Zion Lutheran Church that we may assume they are the work of the same builder.

This Roman Catholic church, the first in the area, served Stratford, but when New Hamburg was settled, most parishioners began to attend church there.

Today it has become mainly a mortuary chapel surrounded by tombstones. It would be hard to find another place where the peaceful atmosphere of the building blends as well with the landscape.

Delhaise 82

St. George's Church, 1888
NEW HAMBURG

ANGLICAN

Since most of the population of New Hamburg was of Germanic stock, the honour of being the first church in the area cannot be given to this Anglican church.

St. George's parish goes back to 1853, when the Rev. Peter Van Linge, the first permanent incumbent, came to Canada from Holland. As no church yet existed, services were held in various homes, halls and barns. The present church was built in 1888 with its entrance lying upon the first English settlement in the south end of the township. In September 1906 a disastrous collision on the Canadian Pacific Railway occurred between a tourist train and a freight train. On the long death list, the largest number from any one place were from New Hamburg and vicinity; the funeral service was the occasion of the largest gathering at St. George's in recent years.

St. George's is also called the Church of the Rainbow, after the two rainbows in the stained glass window over the altar, a unique feature in this part of Canada.

Delhaise 81

St. Agatha Zion
Lutheran Church, 1863
ST. AGATHA

LUTHERAN

The similar sizes, proportions and styles of St. Anthony of Padua and St. Agatha lead us to believe that the same builder probably constructed both. The two churches' similarities are characterized by the their sturdy structures.

St. Agatha's first pastor was the last post of Rev. D.S. Binderman. Born on July 1, 1790, in Prussia, he served as a rifleman in the Prussian army and came to Waterloo in 1834. At his first church his liberal universalist leanings caused conflicts and, by public demand, he was replaced by a conservative Lutheran in 1835. He moved around, founded several churches and was always sent away. He founded St. Agatha, his last church, in 1863. Here, too, he met with dissension, resigned, and was replaced in 1864. Dejected and disappointed, he died the following year.

Delhaise 84

Speedside United Church, 1855
ERAMOSA

UNITED

The first United Church congregation of Eramosa was founded in 1845. New members were submitted to strict examinations before being accepted, and if they drew wheat on Sunday, they were severely disciplined. Ten years later, on October 3, 1855, Speedside church opened its doors to the community.

Like many other buildings in the Guelph area, this unusual octagonal church was built with stones. Its shape may have originated from the post-Reformation polygonal churches in Scotland. The story goes that, built as close to a round shape as possible, the devil could not hide in its corners. To furnish this unusual-shaped church, the pews were made to almost surround the pulpit, allowing us to recall the early years when the ministers could not escape the harsh eyes of the congregation, or vice versa.

Delhaise 82

Acton Baptist Church, 1900
ACTON

BAPTIST

Residents of Acton gathered in 1842 to establish a Baptist Church. In 1856 a service of recognition was held in which delegates from Cheltenham, Georgetown and Guelph proclaimed the church as the Regular Baptist Church of Acton. Two years later the first church building was erected.

A loyal parishioner, Miss Steele, gave the land in 1896 for the church which still stands today. Mr. J. Francis Brown, the well-known church architect, built this church, which was completed and formally dedicated in 1900.

Delhaise 80

St. Stephen's Church, 1837
HORNBY

ANGLICAN

This fine example of pioneer Canadian church architecture was built from the timbers cut in the bush across the road. Members of the first congregation started their work of chopping trees and preparing lumber a year before the doors opened. Their industry and skill are proven by the sturdy, well-built structure and the original clapboard siding, which have survived 150 harsh Canadian winters.

The first service was held in 1837 and Bishop Strachan of Toronto consecrated the church on July 14, 1862.

Entries in the records show that the congregation raised large families, with as many as 17 or 18 children baptized in the church.

ST. STEPHEN'S CHURCH AND CEMETERY

Delhaise 83

Christ Church, Est. 1842
WOODBRIDGE

ANGLICAN

Being on the Humber River, this area served as a chief thoroughfare to and through the Huron Country in the sixteenth and seventeenth centuries. The first church, destroyed by fire in 1921, was replaced within the year. Pieces of the old bell were collected and remodelled, and a finer, more musical unit took its place in the empty tower.

On the west side of the church stands a window of great historical value. The Rev. N. Clarke Wallace, while serving as a chaplain in World War II, collected pieces of stained glass from bombed churches and cathedrals all over England (Westminster Abbey, Canterbury, St. Paul's and St. Martin's in the Field, London, Coventry, etc.) and brought them to Canada to make this unique window.

Delhaise 82

St. Paul's Presbyterian Church, 1906
LEASKDALE

PRESBYTERIAN

The people of Leaskdale organized St. Paul's Parish in 1862. Two years later they built a frame church on a piece of land donated by George Leask. Because of the small size of Leaskdale and Chalmers in Uxbridge, they became one charge and remained together until 1880.

The lancet windows of the new yellow-brick church built in 1906 give this sturdy building an elegant Regency look.

The Rev. Montgomery served as a minister from 1911 to 1926. Along with him, he brought his wife, L.M. Montgomery, famous author of *Ann of Green Gables*. In this picturesque village she wrote half of her 22 novels.

Delhaise 81

14

St. Andrew's-Chalmers
Presbyterian Church, 1884
UXBRIDGE

PRESBYTERIAN

In the 1850s there were many Presbyterian "Free Church" supporters who broke away from the American Methodists. They wanted, among other things, a say in choosing their own pastors.

In Uxbridge, worshippers went to the Wesleyan Methodist Church. The two groups held a Union Sunday School until 1868, but both felt more and more a need for their own quarters. The Presbyterians then erected a small church in 1869.

This soon became too small, and in 1884 the actual church was built, a surprisingly happy mixture of architectural styles. The Roman window above the front door was artistically divided in two ogival lights, thus matching the other windows, but the drip mould above it repeats the "down to earth" Roman arch.

In 1921 the pastor of Chalmers also ministered St. Andrew's at Quaker Hill. When St. Andrew's closed, an addition was made at Chalmers and it was renamed St. Andrew's-Chalmers Presbyterian Church.

Delhaise 81

Wick Presbyterian Church, 1893
SUNDERLAND

PRESBYTERIAN

Dr. Robert Burns, appointed by the presbytery of Toronto to dispense services to settlers, established an organization called "The Wick Presbyterian Church" on February 17, 1849. The Rev. John Mitchell, ordained in 1853, was the first settled minister at Wick. He supervised building the original frame church.

In 1892 the congregation decided to replace the wooden church and within a year erected the present church, a red-brick construction of Norman character with pinnacle-topped buttresses and a beautiful rose window.

In 1924, when the idea of church union with the Methodists was proposed, the Wick's members preferred to remain part of the Presbyterian Church of Canada.

Delhaise 82

All Saints Anglican Church, 1871
CANNINGTON

ANGLICAN

"Of all the villages and towns of the county," read a nineteenth-century article on Ontario County, "Oshawa and Cannington have the brightest industrial future." The coming of the automobile gave favour to Oshawa. Today Cannington is best known for its native Robert Holmes, noted botanist and artist, born in 1861. Holmes became a respected teacher at Upper Canada College and at the Ontario College of Art. He died delivering a graduation address at O.C.A.

Regular Church of England services began in the Cannington neighbourhood in 1835, usually in barns. As the community of Cannington grew, members of the St. Thomas congregation thought of building a church in the village and changed the name from St. Thomas to All Saints. The construction started and on December 17, 1871, the opening service of the new church was held.

In 1884 a fine English fence was constructed around the church, but it is believed that during World War II, the fence was melted down for munitions.

Delhaise 80

St. George's Church, 1876
JACKSONS POINT

ANGLICAN

Jacksons Point's first church, built in 1838, was replaced by St. George's 38 years later. Perpendicular windows on the sides, a battlements-topped bell tower and a beautiful pattern of stonework give this little church a strong Gothic character.

Captain Thomas Sibbald, a colourful personality, supervised the 1876 construction. He introduced naval practices to the job site, appearing each day at "eight bells" to issue the rum ration and supervise the toast to the Queen. He insisted that his remarks be replied to with "Aye, aye, sir." If the workers objected, they hid their feelings and, because of Captain Sibbald's expertise, followed his seafaring commands.

The well-known writer Mazo de la Roche, author of the famous *Jalna* series, died in 1961 and is buried in the west end of the churchyard by Lake Simcoe.

Delhaise 85

Christ Church, 1862
ROCHES POINT

ANGLICAN

In 1857 the principal of Upper Canada College in Toronto had a serious breakdown and was forced to retire and stay at his parents' farm in Roches Point. This move proved very beneficial to his recovery and to Roches Point. It was he, the Rev. Stennet, who designed Christ Church and had it built in 1862 with local field stones.

The elegant open bell cote gracefully enhances the charm of this rural English-style church. The well-trimmed landscape invites you to rest, and a bench is even provided by the door.

Delhaise 82

19

St. Thomas' Church, 1838
SHANTY BAY

ROMAN CATHOLIC

In 1838 Lt.-Col. Edward O'Brian, leading member of the Shanty Bay settlement, gave a piece of land for the erection of St. Thomas' Church. He directed the Italianate-style building to be made of "rammed earth," a mixture of clay and chopped straw. When dry, the structure was covered with plaster. There are few buildings of this type still standing in Ontario, and St. Thomas' is probably the only church of this construction still in use.

Lucius O'Brian, the second son of St. Thomas' designer, was an Ontario artist of distinction in the late nineteenth century.

Delhaise 83

20

Chapelle Sainte Marie, 1639
SAINTE-MARIE-AU-PAYS-DES-HURONS
(MIDLAND)

ROMAN CATHOLIC

The very short story of Sainte Marie lasted only ten years. In 1639 French missionaries went to Huron country to establish a village where priests could rest after hard work among the natives in distant settlements.

For years the Huron were at war with the Iroquois over the fur trade. In 1648 the Iroquois attacked the nearby village of St. Joseph. The next year the aggressors captured hundreds of Hurons as well as Fathers Jean de Brebeuf and Gabriel Lalemant. Finally the Jesuits decided to burn Sainte Marie and leave for the Christian Island, then for "Kebec" in 1650.

Chapelle Sainte Marie was built under the direction of Father Lalemant according to the design of Charles Boivin, resident master builder, and his assistant, Guillaume Couture, both from Rouen, France. The roof was shingled with elm bark in the Iroquoian way.

The village and the church have been restored and show an unique example of life in the middle of the seventeenth century.

Delhaise 84

21

St. George's Anglican Church, 1880
MAGNETAWAN

ANGLICAN

Built in 1880 on rock, this church served as a centre for the Anglican mission. On October 2, 1881, loyal parishioners rowed 13 miles through a storm on Lake-Se-sebee to have their children baptized at St. George's. The little church did not serve many, and as the new minister, Rev. W.F. Smith, said upon his arrival in 1921, "The faithful are few." But when leaving five years later, he admitted, "The few are faithful."

The actual congregation of about 20 members increases greatly in the summer months with the influx of tourists, mostly Americans. That is why since August 29, 1953, the Stars and Stripes have hung alongside the Union Jack inside the church.

In 1933 A.J. Casson, the last living member of the Group of Seven, did a painting of St. George's and titled his work "The Church on the Rock." This well-known work hangs in the National Gallery of Canada.

Delhaise 86

22

Madill Church, 1872
HUNTSVILLE

WESLEYAN METHODIST

One outstanding characteristic of the Methodist Church was its ability to establish itself in newly settled areas. Just one example of this is Madill Church, south of Huntsville. In 1872 John Madill Sr. donated an acre of land for a church and a burying ground. While still building their own homes and clearing the land, the congregation constructed the church, with each family giving two rounds of logs.

The Rev. Thomas Snowden was the first minister in charge, and the first person to rest in the new cemetery was John Madill's daughter, who died in 1875.

The pioneers who built this church with love and sacrifice now rest in the well-maintained cemetery surrounding the old log church. This resting place is one of quiet beauty, dignity and peace.

To my knowledge, this is the only log church remaining in the province. It is no longer used regularly, but the United Church of Canada holds an annual service here.

23

St. Luke's Church, 1903
BURNT RIVER

ANGLICAN

It has been suggested that the name Burnt River comes from the fact that the Indians burned everything behind them when they left the region. But most probably the culprits were the lumbermen who over-cut and burned the brush in the district's once beautiful hardwood and white pine forests.

Under the direction of Mr. Shuttleworth, the stonemason, the Anglican parishioners gathered for a work bee and in one day quarried and carried the stones for the construction of St. Luke's.

This tiny rural sanctuary, with its charming miniature belfry, was extended in 1967 by a matching front porch.

Services are still regularly held here at St. Luke's, in this peaceful hamlet.

Delhaise 83

24

St. Mary's Church, 1867
YOUNG'S POINT

ROMAN CATHOLIC

The history of Catholicism in Lakefield began with the arrival of a number of French Canadians attracted to the lumber business. In 1825 Francis Young, his seven sons and two daughters, settled at the junction of Clear Lake and Lake Katchawanooka. Once the land was cleared and the harvest proved bountiful, Young built a combined saw and grist mill on the natural waterfall between the two lakes.

By 1865 Francis, the third son of Francis Young Sr., had donated land for a church and the present village of Young's Point received its name.

The church, dedicated to Our Lady of Good Counsel, was completed in 1867. In 1898 Young's Point Mission was raised to parish status with Lakefield as a mission; two years later Keene became another mission of Young's Point. Because of dwindling population in the area, St. Mary's returned to mission status in 1901 and has remained that way.

The delicate spire and pinnacles of the belfry give a note of elegance to this otherwise simple building.

Delhaise 81

25

Christ Church, 1853
LAKEFIELD

ANGLICAN

A group of English gentlefolk who were very active in the Romantic literature movement instigated the building of Christ Church. The artistic community chose this picturesque location near the water and hired the famous church architect Kivas Tully.

Enamoured with the area, Tully remained and married the daughter of Colonel Samuel Strickland of Lakefield. Tully later became the official architect for the Government of Canada and is known for such works as the Osgoode Hall additions in Toronto and Victoria Hall in Cobourg, to name but two.

The minute Gothic stone church with sturdy buttresses has a beautiful mullioned stained-glass window lighting the altar from behind.

Delhaise 81

26

Church of St. Jude, 1848
SCARBOROUGH

WEXFORD PRESBYTERIAN

St. Jude's first burial (three-month-old Edward Parkin) goes back to March 22, 1832. He was the son of Mrs. Ann Parkin, who donated the land 16 years before the church was erected on the cemetery grounds.

The Church of St. Jude, built with beams cut to simulate the stone used in the original church in England, is still one of the treasures of Scarborough. The steeple, built in York, now Toronto, took several days to be carried by sleigh to Scarborough. Today this seems an unreasonable length of time, but we must remember that in those days life differed greatly from our present day standards: roads meandered through meagrely cleared forests, cooking was often done in the open, and wolves roamed freely near new dwellings.

In 1929 stained glass windows were installed, together with a new altar, but the outside has not changed. This tiny white gem still stands today, thin spired on the green hillside.

Delhaise 86

27

St. Paul's on the Hill, 1934
DUNBARTON

ANGLICAN

Originally called The Church of the Ascension, this church was located at 131 Richmond Street West in Toronto. The architect, Stewart Strickland, built it in 1877 in the modified Gothic style using bricks and stones. In December 1933 the church was disestablished, and the next year workers dismantled and reassembled the church on private property in Dunbarton. It was dedicated by Archbishop Owen as St. Paul's on the Hill on November 16, 1934. The Anglican Church has owned the land since 1976, when Mr. Harry Newman deeded the church property to the incumbents and church wardens. St. Paul's was then consecrated on March 21 by Archbishop Lewis Garnsworthy.

Delhaise 81

28

St. George's Anglican Church, 1841
PICKERING

ANGLICAN

Since 1826 the Anglican Church had missions in Pickering. St. George's parish was founded in 1832 and a church was built in 1841. The Grand Trunk Railway paid for the bricks for St. George's in exchange for the right of way through the church property, which extended much further south at the time.

Flanked by sturdy buttresses, this austere construction is lightened by elongated windows and a delicate open belfry straddling the very steep roof.

Much to the dismay of present-day historians, the church records were lost in 1925.

29

St. John's Episcopal Church, 1836
WHITBY

ANGLICAN

Port Whitby was a grain centre when St. John's was built; grain was shipped to many places, including Kingston, where it was replaced by a ballast of limestone cut by prisoners. The ship then returned to Port Whitby, unloaded the limestone, and began another trip to deliver grain. One of the most important buildings in the area to be built with the limestone was St. John's.

On May 27, 1872, the church was struck by lightning and badly damaged, especially the east wall, which was repaired much later in 1913. During the reconstruction, a mystery was solved. Some time earlier, someone had given an article of decoration that was considered offensive to the "low" church people, so somebody apparently conceived the brilliant idea of thrusting the "horrid" object between the crevices of the east wall. Whatever it was, this mysterious article, when found in the broken wall in 1913, disappeared just as mysteriously as it had before.

The cemetery is much older than the church. It was consecrated at an unknown date by Bishop Strachan of Toronto.

Delhaise 81

30

St. Thomas' Anglican Church, 1869
BROOKLIN

ANGLICAN

St. Thomas' Church was built in 1869 by George Conway according to plans by the noted Canadian church architect Henry Langley. In 40 years, Langley designed over 70 churches, among them the lovely St. Peter's (Carlton Street, Toronto), All Saints (Whitby), St. Patrick's (William Street, Toronto), and the bell chamber and spire of St. Michael's Cathedral (Toronto).

St. Thomas' Anglican Church used to be referred to as "The Little White Church." High and low points dot the history of St. Thomas'. On New Year's Eve 1899, the rector rang the bell with such energy that it fell and hauled him to the ceiling. He was later discovered on the floor seriously injured. Records neglect to say whether a service was held that New Year's Day.

The short-sightedness of the congregation caused perhaps the greatest disaster. In 1901 they purchased a very expensive marble baptismal font and then, because of lack of funds, had to close the church for three years and worship with the Presbyterians.

Delhaise 81

31

Church of the Ascension, 1868
PORT PERRY

ANGLICAN

In the middle of the nineteenth century, all denominations in Port Perry worshipped in a furniture shop. Mr. J. Perry, a merchant of Port Whitby, donated land for the erection of an Anglican church, which opened its doors on February 25, 1868. Rumour has it that in January 1867 the roof blew off, probably during construction, and the bell fell down. It was replaced by another one from Greenbank.

The Church of the Ascension was consecrated 18 years later, on May 5, 1886, after it was fully paid for, thus following the Anglican custom. It is said that the pews of the Church of the Ascension faced the centre until 1950, when they were replaced and positioned in the traditional manner. The very beautiful rectory, in the same style as the church, was built in 1905.

Delhaise 81

32

St. Paul's Anglican Church, 1876
BETHANY

ANGLICAN

In May 1876, J.K. Kerr, Grand Master of the Grand Lodge of Canada, officiated at the laying of St. Paul's cornerstone. Many members of the Masonic Orders of Port Hope, Lindsay and Peterborough witnessed the ceremony, then attended the opening service on November 12, 1876.

This red-brick church of harmonious proportions is flanked by an elegant tower decorated with brackets supporting the steep pyramidal-louvred spire in which a bell was installed in 1903.

Two box stoves were needed to heat the church until 1925, when a wood-burning furnace was installed. This was replaced in 1951 by an oil furnace.

Delhaise 83

33

Trinity of the Marsh, 1876
MILLBROOK

ANGLICAN

This modest, charming little church stands today exactly as it did over 110 years ago. The congregation worshipped in a schoolhouse for some time, but through the generosity of James Fallis, who donated the land, they were able to build a church.

The slender, perpendicular lines of clapboard siding give it a touch of delicacy not to be found in the more popular brick churches in the area. Flower services were a yearly affair held in the summer. On that day the children marched into the service carrying large bouquets of flowers to be sent to the Sick Children's Hospital in Toronto. In 1969, 200 people attended the flower service.

The smallest in the neighbourhood, Trinity of the Marsh has always been dependent upon the larger churches, sometimes doing without a full-time rector. Today Trinity of the Marsh still serves the community, and two ministers share duties between six churches.

Delhaise 83

34

St. Paul's Anglican Church, Est. 1818
CAVAN

ANGLICAN

Until 1856 people worshipped in a small log structure known as St. Paul's. Today's frame church stands in the same spot on the 4th Line in Cavan, about two miles from Millbrook, but it is not used regularly. Entirely covered with cedar shingles, this tiny building boasts sturdy buttresses, elegant lancet windows on the facade and a delicate wrought-iron lightning rod.

In 1853 the Rev. Thomas Wm. Allen was the third rector appointed to Cavan. His 52 years of service was the longest rectorship on record. In addition, he became Archdeacon of Peterborough and served this post until his death in 1905.

Delhaise 83

35

Grace Presbyterian Church, 1897
MILLBROOK

PRESBYTERIAN

In 1816 John Dyell came from Ireland, built a grist mill by a brook and thus laid the foundation for the town of Millbrook. The town grew steadily and developed a cultural setting for the residents. In fact, in 1875 Millbrook organized the Light Cavalry Band, one of the first mounted bands in Canada.

The plans for Grace Church were decided upon after parishioners viewed the Presbyterian church in Fenelon Falls. In 1896 the cornerstone was laid and inside is sealed the history of the congregation. The official opening, on January 17, 1897, was met with gratitude, for the congregation had waited, saved and worked many years for this church. It is remarkable that this impressive church, with its Italianate mullions and its elaborate brick pattern, was constructed in four and a half months for under $4,000.

Delhaise 83

36

Hiawatha United Church, 1870
KEENE

UNITED

Hiawatha ("he makes rivers") is a legendary North American Indian chief who symbolizes civilization and progress and serves as a magical protector of mankind against the evil forces of nature.

The original mission in the area began in 1825. Among its most notable missionaries were Peter Jones, the first Indian convert of the Methodist Church of Upper Canada, and James Evans, the inventor of the Cree alphabet. Through their work a small but strong congregation formed, and to meet their needs a church was built in 1870.

On the banks of Rice Lake, this tall weatherboard church is still heightened by an elegant three-tier square tower topped by an octagonal steeple.

37

Shiloh Church, 1891
NEWTONVILLE

WESLEYAN METHODIST

In 1860 the people of Sackville decided that their community needed a church. One year later their plans were fulfilled and the congregation attended the opening service at the Shiloh Church.

The elongated spire with its louvred lancets contrasts sharply with the sturdy square tower of this red-brick church. It was raised in 1914 and a basement was added. To the horror of the churchgoers, the crowd was too heavy for the new floor and part of it fell. Although many were injured, everyone recovered and a new floor was built to withstand the previously unimagined weight.

Delhaise 82

38

Morrish United Church, 1865
MORRISH (WELCOME)

UNITED

Overlooking Highway 2 near Welcome, Morrish Church was one of the first drawn (in 1983) for this book. Today this typical country church has been demolished.

Around 1850 the English and the United Empire Loyalists moved to this district. Through the industry of the villagers the area flourished, and in 1865 John Morrish and his wife were thought to have donated the land for the church. But at the time of amalgamation, in 1969, it was found in the registry office that they had actually sold the land.

The frame structure was later bricked and a steeple added. A centre of many activities, the church hosted strawberry festivals, honey festivals, dramatic clubs and many more community functions before its destruction a few years ago.

No one seems to know why the Morrish community was called Charlecote at one time, although one elderly resident thought it had to do with some writer. There is a Charlecote in England, near Shakespeare's home, and perhaps it is from there that this name comes.

Delhaise 83

39

St. Andrew's Church, 1844
GRAFTON

UNITED

The Presbyterians built St. Andrew's in 1844. Its style can be compared with the Scottish post-Reformation period around 1600.

In 1925 the Presbyterians and the Methodists completed 23 years of meetings and discussions, and their merger to form the United Church of Canada was completed. The same year, by vote of the congregation, St. Andrew's became one of the first churches to join the new church denomination.

Coming up the maple-lined drive, one is delighted by the lovely silhouette of this charming church, interesting in shape and meticulous in details. The steeple is remarkable in its dainty wooden pinnacles and battlements surrounding its octagonal spire.

Delhaise 83

40

St. Mary's Church, 1875
GRAFTON

ROMAN CATHOLIC

In 1874 Catholics in Grafton desired to form a parish and their wish was fulfilled within a year. First, their application was granted, then one of the settlers, Thomas Heenan, donated approximately four acres of his farm for a church.

This elegant yellow-brick church stands smartly on the hilltop, and its graceful octagonal gold spire can be seen from miles around. The cornerstone containing its original documents was laid on August 12, 1875. These documents, some of them quite damaged by dampness, were taken out in 1935 and deposited later in the Diocesan Archives. The following is an excerpt from these documents: "The Protestants of all denominations contributed liberally towards the fund for the erection of the Church."

Delhaise 83

41

St. Francis de Sales, Est. 1942
COLBORNE

ROMAN CATHOLIC

In 1942 the estate of Dr. Willoughby was sold for the establishment of St. Francis de Sales. His Colonial house was transformed into a church, which means that a Roman Catholic church is now in every community along Highway 2 from Toronto to Belleville.

In December 1942 Monsignor O'Sullivan, Vicar Capitular of the Diocese of Peterborough, blessed the chapel and celebrated the first mass. The parishioners of St. Francis held woodcutting bees to clear the front lawn. The money raised by the sale of the lumber was used to pay for two "I" beams, which were installed on concrete pillars to support the second floor. On top of the tower, the first cross in Colborne was set in place in 1943.

Delhaise 85

42

Prospect Missionary Church, Est. 1937
COLBORNE

UNITED MISSIONARY

The Missionary Church (originally known as Mennonite Brethren in Christ Church) was started in Colborne by the Stouffville Mennonite Brethren in Christ Church. The first meeting was held January 10, 1937, in an upstairs room of the Old Opera House in Colborne. Later a vacant place of business was remodelled to hold church services, but a more suitable building was needed for the growing congregation. In 1948 the Walker Estate — which bore the appearance of once being a church long ago changed into a dwelling — was purchased and changed back into a church.

The name Prospect was taken from a white slab in front of the building bearing the name "Prospect House." In 1968, due to a merger of the United Missionary Church with the Missionary Church Association, it was decided by the revised denomination to rename it "Missionary Church."

Delhaise 83

43

Salem United Church, 1861
SALEM

UNITED

The simplicity of this little church reflects the spirit of the farming community and its priorities.

The founding families of Salem Wesleyan Methodist Church were primarily United Empire Loyalists. As far as we can determine, the original Crown Grant issued in the district went to Colonel John Peters of Vermont. Today his descendants still attend the church, as do the descendants of other persons figuring in the deed. The Methodists have now joined the United Church of Canada.

In 1952 the congregation had electricity installed — referred to by many as an "unnecessary luxury." The church was still heated by a wood stove until 1957.

Of all the small churches proscribed for closure and demolition during the sixties and seventies, Salem was the only one to protest, survive and flourish. It was designated a Heritage Site in 1979.

Delhaise

44

St. Paul's Church, 1862
BRIGHTON

ANGLICAN

In 1862 the Grand Master of the Grand Lodge of Free and Accepted Masons laid the cornerstone of this church in Brighton, which derives its name from "Britheln," an early Anglo-Saxon bishop. In 1911 Bishop Sweeney consecrated St. Paul's, then known as "The Little White Church on the Hill."

St. Paul's elegance rests in the simplicity of its lancet windows and its thin spire over a high bell tower. A fire in 1914 destroyed the church's early documents, so little is known of its history.

Delhaise 84

45

St. John's Church, 1885
CARRYING PLACE

ANGLICAN

The original church in Carrying Place (the well-known portage between the Bay of Quinte and Weller's Bay) was erected in 1824. Very little is known of its history, as the records probably burned with the church. It was replaced in 1885 by the present building. This picturesque church has no formal architectural style, but the high, pointed doors and windows matching the steep roof give this lovely church class, which compensates for its sturdy construction, capable of holding over 400 worshippers.

In the fall the church sheds housed the community's fowl suppers, and in the winter they accommodated about 20 horses and buggies or sleighs.

Delhaise 83

46

Holy Trinity Anglican Church, 1847
CONSECON

ANGLICAN

The name Consecon comes from "Con-con," the Indian word for pickerel, a fish once abundant in Consecon Lake.

A handsome stone church, Holy Trinity has a Norman tower surmounted by a wooden crown of thorns, which is unusual for this part of the world. Regular services were held until 1968, at which time it was the oldest Anglican church still in use in the country.

Today this historical building is preserved as a public library. Sitting on original pews one can enjoy perusing one's favourite books in a peaceful atmosphere with good lighting filtering through the graceful original windows.

47

Rose Hall United Church, 1874
HILLIER

UNITED

The present church replaced an old wooden building called Raynor's Creek Church.

Decorated with rounded windows and door in the Italianate style, it was built with bricks shipped from Cooksville to Trenton by train, then hauled by the local farmers from Trenton to Rose Hall with teams and wagons. The active community regularly used the shed to house chicken-pie dinners, as well as to shelter 24 horses on Sundays.

Church services continued until 1954, and Sunday School until 1963. In the early days Rose Hall was an appointment of the Consecon charge and later of the Wellington charge.

Delhaise 85

48

The West Lake Church of Christ, 1863
WEST LAKE

REFORMATION

Americans who formed Churches of Christ in the Cherry Valley and Hillier areas introduced the Restoration movement to Prince Edward County in 1835. These congregations first met in log houses, schoolhouses, barns and groves. In 1861 Minard and Cathrine McDonald granted land for the West Lake Church of Christ, which was completed two years later.

Although remodelled and enlarged in 1908, the original structure is still in use today by many direct descendants of the original founding families. Of particular note is the lighthouse-style steeple.

49

Christ Church, 1870
KINGSTON (CATARAQUI)

ANGLICAN

The small village of Waterloo (population 75 in 1833), near Kingston, changed its name to Cataraqui, for the Cataraqui River.

In 1811, when John MacDonald was five years old, he emigrated with his father from Glasgow and settled in Kingston, which was to become the capital of Canada from 1841 to 1844. Sir John A. MacDonald, the first Prime Minister of Canada, from 1867 to his death in 1891, was buried in the cemetery of Christ Church in Cataraqui.

Built in 1870, Christ Church was consecrated on October 16 of the same year. By 1878 the congregation had grown to such a size that the church had to be lengthened by 20 feet. The builders managed to achieve unity by using the same material — local limestone — and the same Regency style. To further commemorate the occasion, an imposing bell tower was added.

Delhaise 86

50

St. Augustine's Anglican Church, 1879
ACTON CORNERS

ANGLICAN

St. Augustine's, named after St. Augustine's Church in Canterbury, England, was one of the 15 churches erected by the Rev. John Stannage in the 15-year period from 1866 to 1880. The steeple regularly came down during winter storms, but was finally replaced in the 1930s by the Cross of Iona, a Celtic cross.

As there is still no electricity in the church, the original pump organ accompanies the hymns. And even though there is a service held every other week, the church continues to be heated by a wood stove.

Delhaise 86

Index of Churches

Bibliography

Blake, Verschoyle Benson, and Ralph Greenhill. *Rural Ontario.* Toronto: University of Toronto Press, 1969.

Braughton, J.W.D. *They Desired a Better Country.* (Not published at time of this printing)

Burley, Agnes. *Clarke Township Eastern Section, Its Place, People & Events.* np 1967.

Byers, Mary, Jan Kennedy and Margaret McBurney. *Rural Roots.* Toronto: University of Toronto Press, 1976.

Cannington Centennial 1878-1978. Cannington Centennial Society Inc., 1978.

Carr, Mrs. Ross N. *Rolling Hills.* Manvers Township Council, 1967.

Day, Frank. *Here & There in Eramosa.* Guelph, Rockwood: Leaman Printing Co., 1953.

Farewell, J.E. *Ontario County.* Belleville: Mika Publishing, 1973.

Lambert, Islay. *Call Them Blessed.* Cannington: Corporation of the Village of Cannington, 1971.

Maclean, Rev. Hugh D. *A Rare Gift Within Its Gates.* Niagara-on-the-Lake: T & C Associates, 1980.

MacRae, Marion and Anthony Adamson. *Hallowed Walls.* Toronto: Clarke Irwin, 1975.

McGillivray, Allan. *The Churches of Uxbridge Scott.* Published by the Author, Zephyr, 1978.

Mika, Nick and Helma. *Places in Ontario.* Belleville: Mika Publishing, 1974.

Mika, Nick and Helma. *Prince Edward County Heritage.* Belleville: Mika Publishing, 1980.

Ondaatje, Kim. *Small Churches of Canada.* Toronto: Lester & Orpen Dennys, 1984.

Stafford, Ellen. *Stratford Around and About.* Stratford: Fanfare Books, 1972.

Theberge, Clifford and Elaine. *The Trent-Severn Waterway.* Toronto: Samuel Stevens, 1978.

Whaley, Ken. *St. Stephen's Church.* Erin: The Boston Mills Press, 1977.

OTHER SOURCES

Anglican Church of Canada Archives, Toronto.

Collins, Muriel. "Saved from the Axe." *Country Estate Magazine,* Summer, 1976.

Department of Travel & Publicity Historical Branch, Toronto.

History of the Churches of Prince Edward County. Picton Gazette Publishing.

Local Church Histories.

Ministère des affairs Culturelles et des Loisirs, *Venez découvrir un siècle différent Sainte-Marie-au-Pays-des-Hurons (1639-1649).*

United Church of Canada Archives, Toronto.

Winter, Brian. "Bell Gave Rector a Shock." Oshawa *Times,* April 30, 1983.

Catherine Delhaise studied the basics of painting in Epinal and Paris, France. In 1975 she began painting professionally, and today her works are distributed in several private and public art collections in Canada and abroad. Her paintings, selected many times by jury, have received several awards and she is especially known for her detailed birds in watercolours. The versatility of her work and her natural gift for instruction are perfectly blended in her secondary career as an art teacher.

Her husband, John, also of European background, has always been interested in art and architecture. He studied the visual arts and music for several years in Brussels and Paris, and has celebrated 30 years in the visual arts. Today, as well as working as a translator, he also manages Catherine's art.

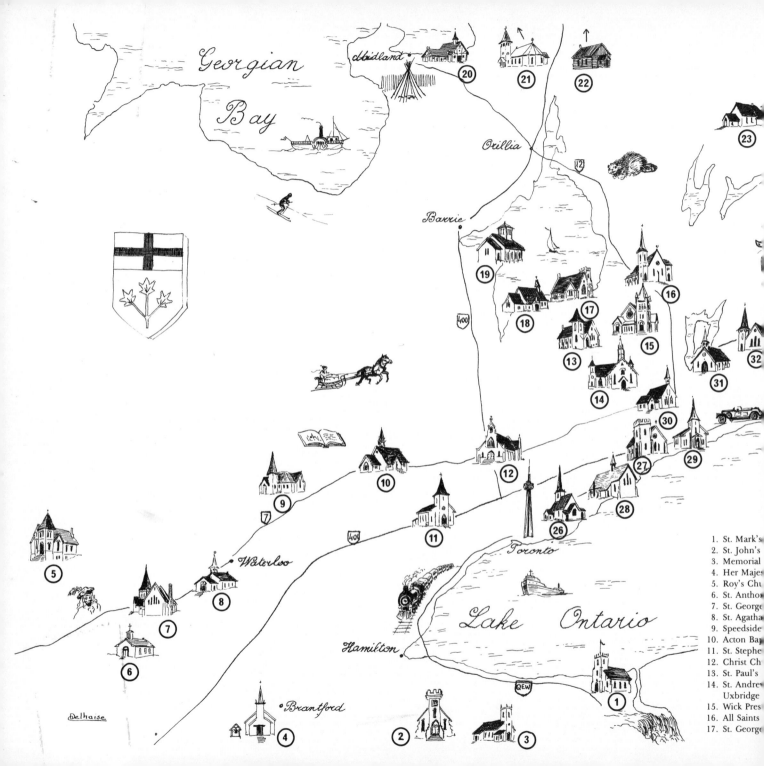

Georgian Bay

Midland

20

21

22

23

Orillia

12

Barrie

19

16

17

18

15

13

14

31

32

400

30

29

27

7

9

10

12

26

28

Waterloo

8

11

Toronto

5

7

Lake Ontario

6

Hamilton

QEW

1

Delhaise

Brantford

4

2

3

1. St. Mark's
2. St. John's
3. Memorial
4. Her Majes
5. Roy's Chu
6. St. Antho
7. St. George
8. St. Agatha
9. Speedside
10. Acton Bap
11. St. Stephe
12. Christ Ch
13. St. Paul's
14. St. Andre
    Uxbridge
15. Wick Pres
16. All Saints
17. St. George